S0-BXX-987

ELEPHANTS

A PORTRAIT OF THE ANIMAL WORLD

Leonard Lee Rue III

SMITHMARK

Copyright © 1994 Todtri Productions Limited. All rights reserved.
No part of this publication may be reproduced, stored in a
retrieval system or transmitted in any form by any means
electronic, mechanical, photocopying or otherwise, without
first obtaining written permission of the copywright owner.

This edition published by SMITHMARK Publishers Inc.,
16 East 32nd Street, New York, NY 10016

SMITHMARK books are available for bulk purchase for sales promotion and premium use.
For details, write or call the manager of specal sale,
SMITHMARK Publishers, Inc.,
16 East 32nd Street, New York, NY 10016; (212) 532-6600

This book was designed and produced by
Todtri Publications Limited
P. O. Box 20058
New York, NY 10023-1482
Fax: (212) 279-1241
Printed and bound in Singapore

ISBN 0-8317-0896-4

Author: Leonard Lee Rue III

Producer: Robert M. Tod
Book Designer: Mark Weinberg
Photo Editor: Edward Douglas
Editors: Mary Forsell, Joanna Wissinger, Don Kennison
Production Co-ordinator: Heather Weigel
DTP Associates: Jackie Skroczky, Adam Yellin
Typesetting: Command-O, NYC

PHOTO CREDITS

Photographer/Page Number

Dembinsky Photo Associates
Mike Barlow 6
Stan Osolinski 5, 16, 28 (top), 77, 79
Fritz Polking 15 (top), 42

Joe McDonald 24 (left), 29, 33 (bottom) 38, 40-41, 43, 48, 50, 53, 58, 73

Nature Photographers Ltd
P. Craig-Cooper 34 (bottom), 45, 63, 73 (bottom left), 74 (bottom)
Paul Knight 68, 74 (top)
W.S. Paton 11
Hugo Van Lawick 14 (top), 44, 54 (top), 60 (top)
Paul Sterry 13, 23

Len Rue Jr 4, 8-9, 36, 60 (bottom), 62 (top & bottom), 67 (bottom)

Leonard Lee Rue III 3, 12 (bottom right) 27, 46, 59

Tom Stack & Associates
Nancy Adams 32 (top)
Walt Anderson 66, 67 (top)
Gerald A. Corsi 22, 30
Warren Garst 20
Barbara von Hoffmann 24-25, 26, 69
Joe McDonald 75
Mark Newman 64
S. K. Patrick 7 (bottom), 35 (bottom)
Inga Spence 39

The Wildlife Collection
John Giustina 28 (bottom)
Martin Harvey 7 (top), 10, 12 (top), 14 (bottom), 15 (bottom), 21, 31 (top & bottom),
32 (bottom), 33 (top), 34 (top), 35 (top), 37 (top & bottom), 47, 49, 51, 52,
54 (bottom), 55, 56-57, 61 (top & bottom), 65, 70, 71, 73 (top left), 78
Tim Laman 17, 18-19, 72-73

INTRODUCTION

*Wildlife is constantly alert to the scents carried on
the air. An elephant holds its trunk high in order to test
the breeze for the scent of food, friends, or enemies.*

O n a hot, clear day in Queen Elizabeth National Park in
Uganda—now called Rowenzori—in August of 1968
I watched four bull elephants feed on the lush grasses
that grew along the placidly flowing Nile River. And what
elephants they were—a patriarch and his three attendants!
The attendants were all large, mature bulls, thirty-five to forty
years of age, but the patriarch was huge, the biggest elephant
I have ever seen, with tusks to match his bulk. My guide, Finn
Allen, who had been raised in East African game parks, said
that it, too, was the largest elephant he had ever seen.

We estimated that the old bull stood at least 3.3 metres (11
feet) high at the shoulder and that he probably weighed over
5400 kilogrammes (12,000 pounds). His tusks were truly
impressive, projecting slightly beyond his outstretched trunk.
They had to be at least 2.75 metres (9 feet) long and weigh in
the vicinity of 90 kilogrammes (200 pounds) each.

No matter how we tried to approach the old bull in our Land Rover to take photographs, one or several of the attendant bulls blocked our passage. With heads and tails held high, they would flap their ears, roll up their trunks, and bluff a charge at us. All of this was accompanied by much shrill trumpeting, certainly one of the most thrilling, spine-tingling sounds in the animal world.

Through all of this, the patriarch continued his feeding. He never looked up; he moved just enough to reach more grass, and totally ignored us. He either didn't care or else was fully confident in the protective action of his attendants. His faith was not misplaced; we could not, at first, even begin to get close to him.

Our solution—and I've found this works with most of the wild creatures I try to photograph in the field—was to sit in plain view and wait until the subject gets accustomed to our presence. We sat. We waited. The elephants soon became accustomed to us, and then we moved in very slowly and got our photographs.

I treasure these photographs. Of the hundreds and hundreds of elephants I've seen and photographed on the many trips I've made back to Africa, none were as large and impressive as that patriarch. The old fellow was in excellent condition, though he had to be at least fifty-five years old. He has, of course, since died—perhaps a natural death or, more likely, was an early target during the strife and wars in Uganda in the 1970s and 1980s. There are reports of a couple of big tuskers living in Africa today, but I don't know as I'll ever see them, much less get pictures of them. What I did photograph on that day twenty-five years ago was the passing of an era.

Fire is such a commonplace occurrence on the African grasslands— whether set by lightning or by man—that most of the animals, including the elephant, pay very little attention to it.

Elephants are capable of eating the 5-centimetre- (2-inch-) long, needle-sharp, steel-strong thorns of the acacia tree without damaging their trunks, tongues, or mouths.

ELEPHANTS OF YESTERDAY AND TODAY

Proboscideoris, Elephant Lineage

The Asiatic elephant, *Elephas maximus*, with its four subspecies—Indian, Ceylon, Sumatran, and Malayan—and the African elephant, *Loxodonta africana*, with its two subspecies—the steppe, or bush, and the forest—are relics of an ancient order: Proboscidea, animals with trunks.

Today's elephants have descended from two diverse sets of ancestors that developed along parallel lines. The age of reptiles—the time when dinosaurs ruled the earth—had just ended, and sometime in the Paleocene epoch (65 million years ago) tapir-like animals called the Moeritheres evolved in Egypt. These proboscideans had a skull and dentition similar to the present-day elephant, and four teeth that appear to be the forerunner of tusks. The second-oldest family is the Deinotheriidae, which evolved in both Africa and Eurasia.

With favourable conditions these creatures,

over the next twenty-six million years or so, spread out across all of Africa, Eurasia, and, eventually, North America and South America. During this slow, but inexorable, expansion, as different climatic conditions and habitats were encountered, various species of proboscideans evolved that enabled each of them to survive under extremely diverse conditions. They were found from the rim of the

This silhouette shows the general characteristics of an African elephant. Note the angular sloping to the top of the head and the sway-backed slope to the spine, which distinguish it from the Indian elephant.

This silhouette of an Indian elephant shows the characteristic rounded dome to the top of the head and the highly arched spine, which are noticeably different from that of the head and spine of the African elephant.

Although their tusks are strong and are intended to be used in procuring food, elephants occasionally snap off a tusk when they are gouging fibres out of a tree trunk or digging up roots.

Following page: Although giving birth to twins is extremely rare, it can occur when the herd size is stable and the food is plentiful.

7

polar ice cap to the edge of the desert, through tundra, taiga, forest, savannah, and swamp. Over three hundred species evolved into four basic lines.

Elephant Ancestors

Deinotherium evolved in the Eocene epoch (58 million years ago), and closely resembled present-day elephants. However, they were slightly smaller in size, had a much shorter trunk, and their two large tusks curved down and back. It is not positively known if these tusks were used for raking in vegetation or for plowing up the earth for roots and tubers. This entire line died out two and a half million years ago.

Gomphotherium evolved in the Oligocene epoch (37 million years ago). They developed an elephantine body, but had only a rudimentary trunk. They had teeth like present-day elephants, but in addition they had four small tusks, two curving up and two curving down. Some members of this group developed wide, flat, shovel-like jaws that enabled them to scoop up the marshy vegetation upon which they fed. Other members had a greatly reduced jaw structure, but developed enormous tusks. This line died out relatively recently, perhaps 10,000 years ago.

From Gomphotheria evolved Mammutidae, often called Mastodons, during the Miocene-Pleistocene epochs (10-12 million years ago).

A mature African bull elephant stands 3 to 3.5 metres (10 to 12 feet) at the shoulder and weighs up to 5400 kilogrammes (12,000 pounds).

The melting snow from Mount Kilimanjaro, Tanzania, seen in the background here, provides a river of water that turns Amboseli National Park, Kenya, into a green oasis that is home to a large number of elephants.

The woolly mammoths were slightly larger than present-day elephants and were protected from the cold by a coat of long, dense, reddish hair and a subcutaneous layer of fat 76 millimetres (3 inches) thick. Their identifiably long tusks curved down, forward, and inward and were used to sweep away the snow that covered the vegetation it fed upon in the northern climates, including the steppes of Eurasia and the prairies of North America.

Present-Day Elephants

The African and the Indian elephant are what remain today of the ancient order of elephants. Earlier work by taxonomists considered the African forest elephant to be a separate species, but this elephant has now been declared to be a subspecies of Loxodonta, as is the bush elephant. At one time the Cape elephant of South Africa was considered to be a distinct subspecies of the bush elephant, but it is now recognised as being one and the same as the bush elephant.

A comparison of the two species will show a number of distinguishing characteristics. The African elephant is much larger than the Indian elephant, with a big bull standing 3 to 3.3 metres (10 to 11 feet) high, or more, at the

A huge male African elephant has an itch in one of those hard to reach places, so he is scratching it by rubbing against a tree.

These creatures were recognisably elephants, but had a stockier body, long tusks, and a long trunk. The mastodon's tooth structure differed markedly from present-day elephants, and they had much smaller ears and a dense covering of body hair. Although mastodons had spread to all of the connected land masses, North America has produced the greatest collection of these skeletons. The mastodons were primarily a forest-dwelling species. They are believed to have survived until early man arrived on this continent, approximately 18,000 years ago.

Elephantidae descended from the mastodons in the Pleistocene epoch (1.6 million years ago) and produced the most familiar of the prehistoric elephant family—*Mammuthus*, the huge hairy mammoths—and the two diverse lines of our present-day elephants: *Elephas* and *Loxodonta*. *Mammuthus imperator*, which inhabited the southern half of North America, was the largest mammoth of all, standing 4.5 metres (15 feet) high at the shoulder. The northern woolly mammoth, *Mammuthus primigehius*, inhabited both the northern half of North America and Eurasia. It existed in large numbers and is the most closely studied of all the mammoths because a number of complete, frozen carcasses have been found and are preserved in their entirety today.

The cleft dome is characteristic of the Indian, or Asiatic, elephant. They can also be identified by the size and shape of their ears, which are sharply triangular with the apex pointing down.

The hair on the end of an elephant's tail may grow to a length of 60 centimetres (2 feet) and often can reach the ground.

Elephants do not like to be exposed to direct sunlight in the middle of the day and will seek sanctuary under whatever trees will provide shade. All of their main activities are carried out during the night or during the periods of reduced heat in the early morning or late evening.

During the dry season, the parched land is churned to a powder by the action of elephants' feet, turning the sunset into an orange haze.

The elephants know exactly where to find the most lush foods in their ranges and at what time of the year they will be available. Animals instinctively know which foods have the greatest nutrition and will favour these over the less nutritious varieties when given the choice.

Elephants follow well-worn trails, in use for centuries, that lead to their favourite watering places. For elephants, as for all creatures, the ability to find water is critical to survival.

shoulder. The Indian elephant may be at most 2.4 to 3 metres (8 to 10 feet) high at the shoulder. The Indian elephant, however, has a stockier build so that big males of both species may weigh up to 5400 kilogrammes (6 tons). The females of both species are smaller than the males in size and in weight, with a large female weighing about 3600 kilogrammes (4 tons). The largest recorded African elephant, now displayed in the Smithsonian Institution, has a shoulder height of 4.1 metres (13 feet 2 inches).

In profile, the African elephant has a sloping, sharply angular head. The shoulders are high and the spine is concave, sloping down and then up to the hips. The Indian elephant has a ridge crossing the skull above the eyes and a bulbous knob on the top of the head. Viewed from the front, this bulbous knob is cleft in the centre. The spine of the Indian elephant is higher in the centre of its back than at either the shoulders or hips.

The skin of both species increases in thickness at different parts of the body, but averages about 2.5 centimetres (1 inch) in thickness. The skin of the African bush elephant has a rough texture, and the skins of the African forest elephant and the Indian elephant are much smoother. Individual characteristics, not species, determine the amount of hair that any particular elephant

might have. They all have hair around their mouths on both the lower and upper jaw, but the amount of hair on the head and body varies considerably.

The African elephant's skin is almost uniformly grey. Some Indian elephants have grey skin and others have a much darker base colour, and many have huge patches of pink skin showing through. When an elephant is wet, its skin appears much darker. Because elephants cover themselves with both mud and dust as a protection against biting insects and the sun, their skins take on the colour of the earth that they make use of. The majority of the elephants in eastern Africa, for instance, appear to have red skin because red clay is so common in that region.

An occasional albino will turn up among the Indian elephants, although there is no record of albinos among the African species. The albino is not pure white but a very light shade of grey, and the animal has reddish-grey eyes.

In years past, maharajahs in India would give an albino elephant to any courtier who had fallen out of favour. Because the white elephant was considered sacred it could not be used for work, thus expending a considerable amount of time and money for no direct benefit. Today anything that is costly but of no benefit is considered a 'white elephant.'

Both the African elephant and the black rhinoceros are descendants of very ancient mammals that originated about sixty million years ago.

It is because of its immense size, and not its aggressiveness, that all of the other animals keep a respectful distance from an elephant.

THE BEAST ITSELF

Eyes and Ears

An elephant's eyes are small in relation to its size. In actuality they are just slightly larger than an adult human's eyes. This small size gave rise to the belief that elephants have very poor eyesight. Because of the placement of the eyes on the head, elephants do not have the binocular vision commonly found in predatory creatures and in man. The eyes are a brownish green, surrounded by long black eyelashes, and they have a protective transparent eyelid, known as the nictitating membrane, in addition to their two regular eyelids. An elephant's large ears and its body block out all vision to the rear and reduce what can be seen on each side. Elephants can see much better in a forest, where the light is low and their eyes are shaded. It has been found that even in sunlight an elephant can detect the slightest motion of anything that moves within 45 metres (150 feet) of it.

The ears of African and Indian elephants differ greatly in size and shape. An Indian elephant's ears are sharply triangular, with the sharp end pointing down. An adult Indian elephant's ears measure about 76 centimetres (30 inches) across the top of the ear and about 76 centimetres from the flattened top to the pointed bottom. The tops of the ears are situated well below the crown of the head and are often folded and, occasionally, bent forward.

Although the ears of the two African subspecies of elephants are similar in shape, those of the forest elephant are somewhat smaller than those of the bush elephant. Frederick Selous, the great elephant hunter, recorded the measurements of the ear of one

When they charge, elephants fan out their ears and either roll up their trunk or hold it to the side to get it out of the way.

19

huge bush tusker as 1.7 metres (5 feet 6 1/2 inches) long and 1 metre (3 feet 3 inches) across. In comparison, the ears of a large male forest elephant measured 1.4 metres (4 feet 6 inches) long and 1 metre (3 feet 3 inches) in width.

The thin skin of the ear is stretched over a cartilaginous framework. In African elephants, the tops of the ears are higher than the withers—the ridge between the shoulder bones—and almost touch. The topmost portion of the ears often fold slightly backward. I have seen African elephants whose ears bent forward in half, from top to bottom, through injury.

The opening to the actual ear canal is covered with dense protective hair. And all elephants' ears are richly endowed with surface blood vessels on the rear portion of the ear. The ears are a major thermoregulation appendage. On hot days, elephants at rest or feeding flap their ears constantly. They are capable of enlarging or shrinking the size of the surface blood vessels according to the ambient temperatures. Blood entering the ear is cooled as much as 6°C (10°F) before reentering the body. Although this does not

appear to be a great difference, it does affect the well-being of the elephants.

A temporal gland in front of the ear emits an exudate that is oily in composition and is characterised by a very strong odor. While much has been written about how the gland becomes most active in large bulls during the breeding season, the stains of the exudate on the faces of many, many elephants have been commonly observed, regardless of the sex or age of the animals. It has been noted, though, that the glands are more active when the elephant is excited, frightened, feels threatened, is sexually aroused, or is proclaiming territorialism. The exudate is as personalised as are our fingerprints and this is a primary means of communication among elephants.

When elephants are marking the boundary of their territories, they rub their temporal gland against trees. When elephants greet each other, they often rub their cheeks together, transferring their scent to one another. Young elephants often touch the tip of their trunk to the temporal gland of much larger elephants for positive identification. The glands grow larger as the elephants grow older.

The ears of the Indian elephant are much smaller than those of the African species. They are pinkish in colour, sharply triangular in shape, and often folded and bent forward.

Elephants have very small eyes relative to their body size, yet their eyesight is good. Their eyes are protected by long, stiff eyelashes.

Tusks and Teeth

Elephants have six sets of grinding molars throughout their lifetime, each set consisting of a single elongated tooth. Each tooth is made up of a series of vertical layers—or laminae—of dentine that are cemented together by a layer of enamel. Each layer of the dentine has its own transverse ridge, which produces the rasp-like surface to the tooth needed to grind rough plant fibres used as food. Unlike most vegetative feeders, who masticate their food in a rotary, or sideward, movement of their lower jaws, elephants chew their food in a forward and back motion. When the sixth and final set of molars is worn down and falls out, the elephant will die because it will no longer be able to masticate its food. Dr. Sylvia K. Sikes did extensive anatomical research on elephants and perfected the system of accurately aging elephants by their tooth wear and replacement.

The first set of molars has five layers of laminae, the second has seven, the third and fourth ten, the fifth twelve, and the sixth—an elephant's last set—has thirteen laminae. The first and second set of molars are in place at the same time, and the first is lost at two years of age while the second is lost at four or five years of age. The third set is lost at ten to twelve years of age, and

An elephant's tusks are actually two elongated incisor teeth located in the upper jaw. The tusks continue to grow throughout the elephant's life. Elephants appear to have a dominant side, or handedness, and use one tusk more than the other in gathering food, resulting in the preferred tusk having a blunter tip and a thicker diameter than the other tusk.

Elephants frequently walk about with their trunk draped over one or both of their tusks.

the fourth is in full usage by about ten years of age. The fifth set of molars is in use between the twenty-third and twenty-fifth years. The sixth, and final, set begins to appear at twenty-five to thirty years of age and is usually worn out completely around sixty years of age. Sixty to seventy years is the absolute maximum for an elephant's life span.

The teeth lie progressively from the rear to the front of the jaw, moved along by the formation of the next tooth pushing from behind. In other words, as succeeding layers of laminae wear out and break off of the anterior part of each molar, the succeeding layers and sets of teeth move up to replace them. After the thirteenth lamina of the sixth molar has erupted from the jaw, solid bone builds up behind it and pushes it along.

Using its trunk, the elephant tears reeds loose from their roots. An elephant can also use its trunk to reach up and pluck fruit or vegetation from the branches of a tree that even the tallest giraffe cannot reach.

As their teeth wear out, old elephants do more of their feeding in the marshlands where the lush vegetation is more easily chewed than the woody, fibrous branches of the woodlands.

When their last sets of molars are disintegrating, old elephants move into swampy areas where the soft, succulent vegetation does not require the mastication that woody plant material does.

Lacking the full complement of incisor teeth that most vegetative feeders have, the elephant cannot bite off the food it ingests. The food must be pulled loose with its trunk and then placed into the mouth with it. I have often seen baby elephants put their trunks into their mother's mouth to see what she is eating or even to remove food from the mouth. As there are no medial incisor teeth in the front centre of either jaw, the baby's trunk cannot be bitten by accident as long as it keeps it in the centre of its mother's mouth.

Judging from the size of its tusks, this young elephant is five to seven years old. Within one year of an elephant's birth, its small deciduous tusk (of about 5 centimetres, or 2 inches) is shed and is replaced with the permanent tusk, which becomes longer and heavier as it continues to grow throughout the elephant's life.

This huge bull's tusks are about 2.7 metres (9 feet) long and probably weigh somewhere in the vicinity of 68 kilogrammes (150 pounds) each.

Utilising the long trunk, elephants can feed on vegetation that is 5 to 5.4 metres (17 to 18 feet) above the ground. This sustenance is beyond the reach of all of the other browsing animals except for the giraffe.

The Trunk

The elephant's trunk is a truly marvelous appendage. It is an elongation of the nose and upper lip and is controlled by about fifty thousand muscles. Elephants can breathe through either their mouth or their trunk while on land. In the water they often submerge completely, breathing through their trunk, which is held aloft like a kind of gigantic snorkel.

The trunk can be lengthened or shortened as desired. A snakelike tracing in the dirt is often noted where an elephant has walked along with its trunk tip pointing backward, dragging along the ground. The African elephant has two opposing "fingers" on the end of its trunk, while the Indian elephant has only one, on the anterior tip. These tips are extremely sensitive. I watched an Indian elephant pick up very small coins that had been thrown on the ground and hand them up to the mahout on his back. The tip of the trunk can be used to pick a small berry or a single blade of grass, while the trunk itself can lift logs weighing over a thousand kilogrammes.

An elephant's trunk can be used in many different ways for securing food. When a big bull elephant extends his trunk straight up, he can pluck fruit, leaves, or branches from a tree higher than the largest giraffe can reach, up to a distance of 6 metres (20 feet) or more above the ground. To get a piece of fruit that is too high to reach, an elephant will wrap its trunk around the tree and shake it vigorously until ripened fruit, or nuts, fall to the ground. If the tree is not too large, the elephant may simply push it over by placing his forehead and the front of its trunk against the tree to break it off or uproot it.

Elephants wrap their trunk around swatches of grass and tear it off as neatly as if cut by a scythe. Many times the elephant will simply grasp the tougher grass with its trunk and pull up the entire plant, roots and all. Then, beating the plant against its leg, the elephant knocks the dirt from the plant's root system. At times, the entire plant, according to the species, will be eaten. At other times the leaves and stalk are eaten and the roots cut off by the molars and discarded. On tough-rooted grasses, the elephant will hold the long grass with its trunk and, using its forefeet, kick the grass loose from the roots.

In an extensive marshland, the fast-growing reeds provide the elephants with an almost unlimited source of food. Elephants can wrap their trunk around swatches of grass and tear it off as neatly as if mowed, and they can also grasp tougher vegetation with the trunk and pull up an entire plant, roots and all.

After tearing its food loose, the elephant uses its trunk to stuff the food in its mouth. While feeding, this is a constant process.

By observing the high water mark on the elephant's skin you can see that it was in water deep enough for it to drink with its mouth. While adult elephants usually drink by using the trunk, young elephants will sometimes kneel and drink with their mouth.

Elephants will often wrap their trunks around small trees and shake them until their fruits or nuts fall to the ground, where they can gather them up and eat them.

The elephant's trunk is an elongation of the nose and upper lip and is controlled by about fifty thousand muscles. This elephant extends its trunk to tear off the branches of a yellow-fever acacia tree.

While bathing, an elephant often completely submerges itself, leaving only its trunk above water acting as a kind of snorkel.

An elephant can suck up to 17 litres (18 quarts) of water into its trunk at once.

An elephant places its trunk in its mouth and blows the water down its throat. Elephants also have the ability to put their trunk into their mouth and extract water from their stomach with which to spray upon themselves in order to cool off.

Water blown out of the trunk, as this Indian elephant displays, makes a very efficient high-pressure shower. Tame elephants frequently spray water at their keepers and at spectators.

Interestingly, elephants can tear off and eat branches from the acacia tree—which have 5-centimetre (2-inch), needle-sharp thorns—without doing any injury to its trunk, tongue, or mouth.

The trunk is also, of course, used for drinking. Young elephants sometimes kneel and drink with their mouth, and older elephants, who may have lost the tip of their trunk to a poacher's snare, have been seen wading into deep water to enable themselves to drink with their mouth. But under ordinary circumstances, the elephant puts its trunk into the water and sucks up as much as 17 litres (18 quarts), after which it places the trunk tip into its mouth and blows the water down its throat. Elephants also put their trunks down their throats and extract water from their stomachs, which they then spray upon themselves or on their young in order to cool off.

Elephants will dust bathe many times each day to insure that their bodies have a protective layer of dust in the constant fight against insects.

Quite frequently after bathing in water, and while the skin is still wet, elephants will blow dust over their bodies as protection against insect bites.

Elephants coat
their bodies with
mud as a protection
against the hordes
of biting, blood-
sucking insects.

While bathing,
this baby Indian
elephant has
taken time out
to eat a trunkful
of water hyacinths.

These young
elephants have
entwined trunks
for a bout of
play-fighting.
It is by such
constant testing
that each ele-
phant learns
its place in their
group's hierarchy
of dominance.

Elephants get a great deal of pleasure out of being in water. The buoyancy of the water takes a lot of weight off an elephant's feet and legs. And they cool off by submerging themselves when they can, or suck up the water and spray it as in a shower. Sometimes, too, elephants shuffle their forefeet back and forth to liquefy the mud so it becomes thin enough to be drawn up into the trunk in order to spray it all over their bodies. They also shuffle their feet on land, creating a dust fine enough to be sucked up and then blown over their bodies. They often spray one another, and tame elephants will frequently spray water upon onlookers or sometimes at their keeper.

Elephants use the trunk extensively in relating with each other. While greeting one another they will frequently entwine their trunks in much the same way as humans shake hands. Young, rambunctious elephants utilise their trunks for bouts of play-wrestling.

An amourous male elephant will caress an estrus female with his trunk, running it all over her body, and gently touch her vaginal area to stimulate her for copulation. Mothers caress their babies with their trunks, and also use them to give their young a whack when they are in need of being chastised. A mother elephant will use her trunk to help push her baby up a steep bank or will reach down with her trunk and pull the baby up an

In the courtship process, the male and female elephants will entwine their trunks and remain motionless for long periods of time.

These elephants, with their trunks entwined, could be either in a sexual embrace or merely jousting. It is only by watching them over a period of time that it can be determined what is actually taking place.

incline. Occasionally a mother elephant will walk behind her little one and steer it in the direction she wants it to go by holding the baby's tail. I have seen elephants try to lift a sick or injured baby, or companion, to its feet by using their trunk and their tusks. And mother elephants have been seen carrying their dead babies for days, using their trunks and tusks. Finally the trunk is used to cover the dead baby as they bury it.

The trunk also can be used as an aggressive weapon, where it is flailed against a rival or predator. If an angered elephant can grasp a predator, such as a lion, tiger, or man, with its trunk, it will either throw the victim a great distance through the air or slam it against the ground. Elephants do not kill their enemies by stomping on them with their feet, but they will kneel on them or crush them against the ground with the upper part of the trunk.

Elephants' very keen sense of smell is also a function of the trunk. An elephant with its trunk held high is not about to charge, although it may do so later. The upward-raised trunk tip moves from side to side,

sniffing the air, as the elephant tries to decipher what it needs to know.

The trunk is frequently raised high also as the elephant trumpets its rage, a sound that is awe-inspiring and can be heard at a long distance. This means of elephant communication is what humans know best. However, it's recently been discovered that elephants communicate between themselves most frequently by producing a deep rumbling sound in the chest and throat that is below the hearing frequency of man. This has only been detected by scientific audio recorders. The machines have picked up these rumbling sounds over distances of 4.8 kilometres (3 miles). An alerted elephant will stop this rumbling and that, in turn, may alert the other members of the herd. These communicative rumblings should not be confused with the gaseous rumblings produced by methane in the elephant's stomach. These latter rumblings can also be heard from a considerable distance, but are well within the hearing range of man. If the brush is thick, one may be able to detect the presence of the unseen elephants by their rumbling stomachs long before they can actually be seen.

Following page: This baby Indian elephant, its older sibling, and their mother show the tight bonds of affection that exist between family groups. Elephants use their trunks extensively in relations with other elephants. When greeting each other, for example, they frequently entwine trunks.

When elephants meet they sniff each other all over with their trunks, allowing them to recognise one another individually.

When an elephant raises its trunk in this fashion, it is actually pulling in scent molecules, trying to identify whatever has aroused its curiosity.

Tails and Toes

An elephant's tail can be, on a big elephant, as long as 1.5 metres (5 feet). The distal third portion of the tail is flattened vertically and has long coarse hairs along its two edges. The hairs may be up to 91 centimetres (30 inches) in length. The tail is used primarily as a fly whisk, but is also a good indicator of emotions. When an elephant is frightened or angry, the tail is raised high in an arc and held that way as the elephant charges or runs off. Adult elephants do not, it should be told, walk in circles holding onto the tail of the elephant in front of them with their trunk, as they have been trained to do in circuses.

Elephants are semi-digitigrade animals, walking on the tips of their toes somewhat in the manner of cats and dogs. This cannot be noticed at a casual glance because the bones are encased in the columnar foot. The African elephant has five toes on each forefoot and

Most folks are unaware of just how long an elephant's tail actually is. The long hairs on the end touch the ground and serve the elephant very well in whisking away flies and other annoying insects.

Elephants used to migrate long distances, in large herds, seasonally following the rains. Today their ancestral ranges have been so broken up by land development that they are forced to live in restricted areas.

four toes on each hind foot. The Indian elephant also has five toes on each forefoot and four toes on each hind foot, but occasionally the hind foot will also have five toes. The location of each toe can be seen in the flat nail or hoof in the front of the foot.

The sole of the elephant's foot is a pad of elastic, compressible fibres that expand as weight is applied. This cushion acts as a shock absorber, allowing the elephant to walk on rocks and rough terrain without injury. The bottom dermis of the foot is heavily calloused with ridges that are as individualistic as fingerprints. Trained trackers can easily follow a single elephant in a herd by its individual footpad markings.

The slight compression helps to distribute the elephant's great weight over a larger area, increasing the surface and diminishing the

Elephants move about a great deal, and will travel 16 kilometres (10 miles) or more in a twenty-four-hour period. This constant movement prevents them from completely destroying the vegetation in a single, small area.

bearing pressure per square kilometre. This adaptation is particularly suitable when the elephant walks on soft marshy areas or mud. As the elephant puts its weight on the foot, it expands so that the elephant does not sink in as deeply. As the weight is taken off the foot, it contracts and is easily withdrawn from the large hole it had punched in the mud.

Because of their great weight, elephants usually move by lifting one foot from the ground at a time. Under unusual circumstances—such as when the elephant raises itself upright in a bipedal position, as in feeding, or copulating—it will bring two feet off the ground.

With their long legs, elephants have a stride of about 2.75 metres (9 feet). Walking alongside an Indian elephant, I was forced to walk extremely fast and would estimate

that they travelled at about 8 kilometres (5 miles) per hour or more. Dr. Bernhard Grizemek has stated that elephants will run at speeds of 15 kilometres (9 miles) per hour. He also related that an Indian bull elephant charged at a sustained speed of nearly 40 kilometres (25 miles) per hour, as recorded on his Land Rover speedometre.

Despite their bulk, elephants are extremely sure-footed and can climb very steep mountainsides without slipping. If they suspect the earth won't hold them, elephants carefully test each foothold before putting their entire weight on it. Sometimes, descending a steep mountainside, they will sit and then slide down, using their bottom as brakes. Additionally, the trunk is used to assist them in climbing about among steep forested hillsides. It must be remembered that Hannibal, the Carthaginian general,

An elephant rises by first extending its front legs and resting its weight on its knees. It then tips forward and heaves itself up on its hind feet.

actually tamed and trained African elephants to traverse the Italian Alps in order to attack Rome. Hannibal was defeated in part because the elephants turned out to be less of a factor than he'd anticipated in the battles that followed. Though they were able to get over the steep mountains, the elephants were greatly weakened by a lack of food and the exposure to extreme cold at the high elevation.

These large animals have been known to become lodged in rocky crevasses or become entrapped between trees, boulders, or other immovable objects, where they die of starvation if unable to rescue themselves from such a predicament.

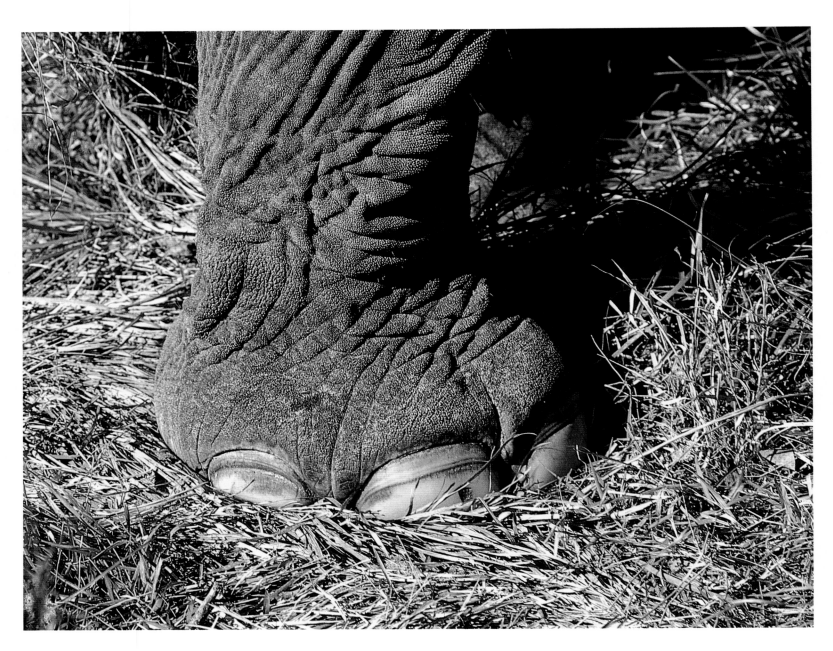

An elephant's toes are actually buried within its foot. Only the position of its toenails on the outer edge of the foot shows where each toe is located.

Elephants frequently rest by raising one foot and crossing it behind another, sort of like humans crossing their legs. The pattern on the bottom of an elephant's foot is as individualistic as a human's fingerprints.

Just prior to copulation the male will caress the female with his trunk, which sexually stimulates her. During courtship the elephants often place the tip of their trunk in their partner's mouth.

With tender loving care, this Indian elephant mother watches over her baby as it bathes in the river.

THE LIFE OF AN ELEPHANT

Reproduction

Elephants usually live in small groups of blood-related families, with a matriarch in charge of the group. The largest old female decides when the herd moves, when it stops, when it feeds, and when it goes to water. She will implement the protective circle when she feels the young in the herd are threatened. She will be the one to charge out of the circle to carry the attack to an enemy if need be.

In both African and Indian elephants, the females are capable of breeding for the first time around their tenth to twelfth year. The gestation period for elephants is twenty-two months. The female is then capable of

breeding again six to eight months later, while her calf is still suckling. This puts a calf-to-calf increment at about twenty-eight months. It was long thought that a cow with a nursing calf could not be bred, but this is not true.

Ordinarily the elephant bulls remain in a herd grouping of their own, but the largest bull in the area may be in close attendance to the cow herd much of the time because as soon as a cow comes into estrus, he will be there to breed her.

It was thought that a male elephant was capable of breeding only when he was in musth, a period of aggressive behaviour accompanied by his temporal glands' high production of exudate. In fact a male is capable of breeding at any time of the year and not just during the four-to-six-week period of the musth. In India, male elephants in musth are not worked, though they are chained securely until that period is over. During musth, the males are extremely truculent, unpredictable, and dangerous. After all the observations and all the studies done over the years, we still don't know what really occurs to the elephant during the musth. As elephants are tropical, or subtropical, creatures, they have no regular breeding season and thus copulation and birthing can take place at any time of the year.

Female elephants have two mammary glands located between their front legs. The male's penis is an impressive organ, as befits a beast of this size. It is usually hidden in the folds of its sheath and curves backward when extended. The testicles are up inside the body. The female's vulva, like the male's penis, is down beneath the hind legs in a sheath. This often causes confusion as to determining the sex of the animal.

The bull, or bulls, are attracted to the cow before she is actually able to be bred. Elephants often display what humans would call tenderness in their courtship. With their trunk, they touch each other all over, gently caressing each other with its tip. As their excitement builds, both male and female give off more temporal scent and this, in turn, acts as a sexual stimulant. The male will approach the female from the rear and gently butt her with his head or tusks. She may then run from him for a brief period. This will be repeated a number of times. When at last she is sufficiently stimulated, she'll bring her rear end toward him and turn her tail to the side and allow copulation to take place.

The male then raises himself up and places his forefeet upon her rump and assumes a squatting position. His penis, which ordinarily curves to the rear, will flex forward and up in a flattened S curve. When the tip of his penis enters the cow's vulva, the bull will rise up on his hind legs so that intromission can take place. The actual length of time of copulation is approximately two minutes. The bull will breed the cow a number of times over the next twenty-four hours.

A male mounts another male not in a sexual act but in order to force the lesser male to acknowledge that the larger male is dominant.

This large African elephant is completely wet, proving that it has either fallen entirely underwater or else sprayed water over its entire body with its trunk.

Dominance

With elephants, as with all animals, the largest, strongest male is usually the alpha, or dominant, male. Such dominance is achieved over a long period of time, as each animal tries to make his way to the top spot. Most frequently, the rivalry between males is settled by contests of strength in a series of play-fighting. Adult animals seldom have to fight because each animal knows his place according to his size. The largest animal can usually maintain his position by offering threat gestures to any of the subordinate animals, which invariably offer in return submissive signals and move out of the way.

Elephants display threat gestures by fanning their ears and shaking their head in a rotary motion that causes both ears and trunk to flop wildly from side to side. The tail is held high and the dominant male will trumpet loudly. A fight does not occur unless the rival is a bull of equal size that has not as yet been tested by his opponent. In a fight elephants crash head to head. Each may flail

Elephants often fan out their ears to make themselves appear even larger to any creature which they believe is a threat. Elephants, like all creatures, try to establish their dominance through threat gestures and only fight as a last resort.

Elephants go through a very elaborate courtship before breeding, and often exhibit what humans would describe as tenderness toward each other.

From the size of the hole this African elephant is standing in you can guess that thousands of elephants, over thousands of years, have taken their dust baths here.

As a threatening gesture, an elephant shakes its head rapidly from side to side, causing the ears to flap.

the trunk or entwine it with that of their opponent. The bull with the longest tusks has the advantage, but if they entwine their trunks neither bull will have a chance to utilise their tusks because the entwined trunks ensure that the opponents fight head to head. Then it becomes a contest of brute strength. The bulls push back and forth until one realizes that the other is stronger. The lesser bull then waits until he has the opportunity to break free without getting gored, whereupon he turns and dashes off. The victor is seldom interested in pursuing the vanquished male. He is boss and he is satisfied with knowing that his rival realises it. The dominant bull's reward is the breeding privileges such rank bestows.

The bull will stay with the cow until her estrus period is over, and then he leaves. He stays in close proximity to the herd while rejoining his old bull herd until another cow comes into heat.

On the plains, where large trees are scarce, elephants will crowd under whatever shade they can find to lessen the heat of the midday sun. As the sun moves, so do the elephants.

Following page:
This is a remarkable photo of a newborn elephant and its mother, along with its three older siblings. Elephants give birth about every third year, beginning from the age of ten to twelve years.

Giving Birth

As her time for giving birth nears, the cow will seek a shady spot in the woodlands or any other comfortable, safe area. She may be alone or she may be accompanied by daughters, sisters, aunts. Unlike most other animals, elephants give birth in the standing position. As the calf slips out of the body, head first, it will tear loose the umbilical cord and remove the placental sac. Any remaining birth tissue is removed by the mother, who carefully runs her trunk over the newborn until it is clean.

At birth a baby elephant weighs between 90 and 115 kilogrammes (200-250 pounds) and stands around 95 to 115 centimetres (38-44 inches) at the shoulders. Within minutes of being born the calf will attempt to get to its feet, aided by its mother. Using her trunk and her tusks, the mother ever so gently lifts her little one. At first the calf's legs are too wobbly to support its weight and it usually falls over backward, but both calf and cow are persistent. Shortly the calf will have attained a sense of equilibrium and takes a few faltering steps. It slowly but surely seeks out its mother's nipple and nurses. The trunk rolls to one side while nursing but later will be held back over its head. At first a calf has little control over its trunk, but it will attain the skill it needs to utilise it perfectly when the time comes to actually have need of it.

Status is very important among all animals. This baby elephant is attempting to dominate one of its older peers.

Baby elephants nurse for a period of up to two years. They begin to eat vegetation almost immediately after birth but depend upon their mother's milk for most of their sustenance.

Like all young-
sters this baby
elephant likes
to go exploring
on its own, but
it will not go far
from the protec-
tion of the herd.

When danger
threatens,
elephants form
a protective
circle with the
babies and young
in the centre.
Elephants exist
in a matriarchal
society and the
protective circle
is initiated by
the dominant
cow elephant.

Baby elephants are born after a gestation period of twenty-two months, the longest gestation period of any land mammal.

By imitating their mothers, baby elephants learn at a very early age about the benefits of coating their bodies with mud.

The two young elephants following the adult cow are twins. This is an extremely rare occurrence in elephants, which usually give birth to a single calf after a gestation period of twenty-two months. An elephant cow may have a calf every two and a half years.

If there are other females in attendance at a birth they too will be as excited by the new-born calf as the mother. They aid in thoroughly examining the calf with their trunks and may also help it to arise for the first time. Because a female elephant herd is basically an extended family, all of the other females, no matter their age, will help with and defend the calf at all times. If any of the other females are lactating, the new calf nurses them as readily as its own mother. Female elephants truly live the dictum "one for all and all for one."

A calf will nurse for a period of up to two years, and sometimes longer, though it will begin to sample various kinds of vegetation within two weeks. By reaching its trunk into its mother's mouth and extracting some of the food that she is eating, the baby soon learns what types of food are best to eat.

Old elephants seldom lie down because it is too difficult for them to get up. Baby elephants will lie down frequently, while middle-aged elephants do so less frequently.

This baby elephant is making threat gestures at some imaginary enemy. If the enemy was real, the mother elephant would be making the gestures. Mother elephants are very devoted to and protective of their young.

*As wild elephants
must actively spend
eighteen to twenty
hours each day
gathering food, they
are usually moving
about all night long.
An adult elephant
will eat between 160
and 180 kilogrammes
(350 and 400 pounds)
of food per twenty-
four-hour day.*

*Elephants eat the
leaves, the twigs,
and the branches—
thorns and all—
while feeding upon
the many types
of acacia trees.*

Eating

Although elephants, including those of the grasslands, are primarily browsing animals, eating a wide variety of bushes, shrubs, and trees, the bulk of their diet is various types of grasses. In many areas of Africa, such as in Tsavo National Park in Kenya and Luangua National Park in Zambia, the elephant herds have become so large that all of their most favoured foods have been eliminated. Thus, in carrying out food studies of any animal today, one must be very careful because the animals may be seen eating other plants than they prefer for these foods are no longer available. Fortunately elephants do eat hundreds of different types of vegetation and when they have the choice will selectively, instinctively pick those foods that provide them with the greatest nutrition.

An adult elephant eats between 160 and 180 kilogrammes (350 and 400 pounds) of food per day. As a result they feed for up to twenty hours each and every day.

Ingesting hundreds of kilogrammes of fibrous material each day means, of course, that an elephant will void hundreds of pounds of feces per day. Elephant feces are pellet-shaped, almost perfectly round, as formed in the intestines—about 13 to 16 centimetres (5-6 inches) in diameter by 16 centimetres or more in length—and they will expel wastes approximately once an hour. Some of the material eaten is changed very little by the digestive process. The pods from the doum palm tree, for example, which elephants love, are virtually untouched after being eaten and voided. Evidently the hard pod is not cracked by the elephant's teeth and is swallowed whole and thus passed out the same way. What benefit the elephants

Elephants can be extremely destructive. Here in the Ngorongoro Crater in Tanzania, elephants have destroyed almost all of the young yellow-fever acacia trees.

Here in Kenya's Amboseli National Park, elephants have destroyed most of the yellow-fever acacias, thus converting what had once been a forest into a desert.

This elephant is pushing against a small tree. It is in this manner that they knock the tree over in order to feed upon its topmost leaves and branches.

actually get out of eating the doum pods is not precisely known, but apparently the pods that have passed through an elephant's digestive system sprout better than those that have not.

Although both African and Indian elephants are creatures of the tropics, neither can stand long exposure to direct sunlight. Because of their bulk, an elephant can stand the cold more than it can the heat. All of their main activities are carried out under the cover of darkness or during the period of reduced heat in the early morning or late in the evening. In Africa, the elephants that have access to a forest will retreat into its cool depths by late morning and not bestir themselves again, if left undisturbed, until mid afternoon. In the more open savannahs, elephants will cluster in the shade of whatever large trees they can find in the area, moving with its shade as the sun races across the sky.

In India elephants are worked only from dawn until late morning and then allowed to rest in the shade until the afternoon. Because the Indian work elephants are fed by their owners, they do not have to spend time searching for food and so can consume what they need in only eight to ten hours.

While humans need an average of eight hours sleep out of every twenty-four, elephants apparently do just fine with four to five hours of sleep a day. However, elephants can be seen frequently to doze off to sleep during the course of a day while they are feeding or relaxing. If the herd is not disturbed in any manner, and the grass is lush, the elephants may close their eyes and eat methodically, mechanically. At such times they appear to actually be asleep. Most elephants sleep while standing, particularly as an elephant gets older. It's simply too difficult for old elephants to get up once they lie down.

The tall papyrus plants in the background nearly dwarf the 3-metre (10-foot) elephants as they feed in a swamp.

It is only after the rainy season, or in a marshland, that an elephant has a chance to feed upon such lush green grasses as seen here.

Drinking

At least once a day elephants go to water. If the water is plentiful and the grasses in the vicinity provide adequate food, the elephants may go to water more often. In Amboseli National Park, the elephants spend almost all of their time in and around the water, constantly feeding back and forth across the great marshes.

Elephants drink up to 76 to 83 litres (20-22 gallons) of water at one time. A big bull may drink as much as 189 litres (50 gallons) per day. Elephants are very sloppy drinkers and lose a lot of the water when they blow it from their trunk up into their mouth. Although a big bull elephant's trunk can hold up to 17 litres (18 quarts) at once, it takes many trunksful of water to slake its thirst.

In times of drought, when the ponds and streams dry up on the savannah, elephants can usually find water by digging for it. They instinctively know, perhaps by smelling it, that they can find water at the dry river beds and so they dig there. Flowing water is usually deepest on the outside of a curve, and in times of drought there is a greater likelihood that water will be found on the outside of the curve; of course that is where the elephants will dig. Elephants dig two different kinds of holes. Some of the holes are great hollows gouged out with tusks and trunks. These large holes are used by all of the other animals in the area as well as the elephants. Some elephant water holes, on the other hand, are only 30 to 46 centimetres (12-18 inches) and are dug out with only the trunk. Other animals trying to use these holes will often collapse the sand walls so that the holes fill in and no water can be had.

Elephants know where every food and water source is in the entire territory in which they reside. They frequently will seek out mineral springs for the minerals contained in either the soil or the water, and eat kilos and kilos of soil for its mineral contents.

Traditionally, elephants had been seasonally migratory. They knew when to leave areas subject to drought before the water tables

A herd of elephant cows and calves slake their thirst. Elephants may drink up to 83 litres (22 gallons) of water at one time.

Because water is such a scarce commodity in most of Africa, the elephants have to share these crucial spots with all other wild creatures. Here a herd of impala drinks in the background.

Elephants were taking beneficial mud baths long before humans mimicked such healthy skin practises.

Elephants will become very playful while in water. This African elephant is stomping with its forefoot just to see the mud and water splash.

After feeding upon the sere, dry grasses in the surrounding countryside, all the animals are pulled toward the available water like iron filings to a magnet.

Wild animals know instinctively that they need various minerals in their diet. This elephant is eating the soil at just such a natural mineral spring, or lick.

Elephants love to bathe, play, and splash around in water. They drink, cool off by sub-merging, and suck up water into their trunks and spray it all over themselves and one another.

dropped to the point where it was difficult for them to drink from it.

Accounts from early explorers tell of herds of elephants over a hundred strong. The animals followed the rains and the abundance of vegetation that such rains produced. Today the elephant herds are fragmented and, although there might be slight seasonal shifts as to where they feed and water, they are basically restricted to certain areas because of the extensive land development surrounding the national parks, where most elephants live today.

I saw the first five elephants to come into the eastern area of Serengeti National Park in Tanzania in 1968. The park warden told me then that elephants had never been seen in that region before. They were being forced into the area by the pressure from human populations in the regions where they had previously lived. The human destruction there was awesome. Even though there were only a few thousand yellow-fever acacia trees in the entire region, many such trees, favoured by elephants, were torn down to make way for development. The loss of these trees caused irreparable harm to the habitat, not only for elephant populations but for lions and leopards, and other animals as well.

The baobab is the largest tree growing in East Africa, some growing to a diameter of 3.5 metres (12 feet). The wood is comparatively soft, and elephants naturally prefer it. Using their tusks, they gouge huge, fibrous strips from the tree. Continuous feeding on the huge tree eventually weakens it and it comes crashing to the earth, whereupon the elephants consume the entire tree. Even the huge stumps will be eaten level with the earth.

Elephants know their home range very well. They know exactly where they can ford this river without having to swim. The intimate knowledge of any animal's home range is a key factor in its survival.

Fascination with Death

A great deal has been written about the so-called elephant's graveyard, an area to which the huge beasts are supposed to retire when they are about to die. Early explorers were said to search for this mythical area because of the wealth of ivory tusks it was presumed to contain. Research has proven that elephants in fact die where they happen to be at the time of their death. Occasionally a number of elephant skeletons are found together in marshy areas, but not because such an area happens to be an 'elephant graveyard'. As mentioned earlier, many old elephants will seek out marshy areas as a food source when their last set of teeth begins to disintegrate. Naturally, more elephants will die in these marshy areas because that's where they last journeyed to prolong their lives with the life-giving softer foods.

Elephants do seem to have a fascination with death. They are caring creatures, and if a member of the herd is sick or injured the other elephants go to great lengths to get their comrade back up on its feet. When death occurs, other elephants in the herd are very reluctant to leave the area of its demise. When a baby elephant dies, the mother and perhaps one or two relatives will stay with the body for several days. Sometimes the body of an elephant is covered over with vegetation by other elephants in an attempt at burial. Whenever elephants come across the bones of even a long-dead elephant, they sniff them over carefully with their trunks. The old bones have been bleached white by the sun and rain over a period of time, and it does not seem possible that there can be an odor left, yet the elephants still inspect them. Occasionally, too, they'll pick up bones and carry them in their trunk for considerable distances.

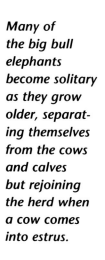

Elephants are fascinated with the skeletons and bones of other, long-dead elephants. Here a pair check out an old elephant carcass.

Many of the big bull elephants become solitary as they grow older, separating themselves from the cows and calves but rejoining the herd when a cow comes into estrus.

The sun is not setting on the elephant as a species. Enough people and their governments are concerned for them, and as a result protective measures have been taken to insure that there will always be elephants.

Afterword

The future of the elephant is largely dependent upon man. Poaching at last has been drastically reduced since a worldwide ban on the sale of ivory went into effect in 1989. In some areas, the ban on the sale of ivory has hurt the countries that were most progressive in protecting the elephants. Ironically, these countries depended upon the sales of the ivory from culled elephants to finance the protection that was provided to the general elephant population.

All too often, because of contemporary circumstances, when elephants are given complete protection they become their own worst enemy. An area cannot support more of any kind of life than there is food available to sustain it. When an elephant population is unchecked it will destroy its range by overgrazing and overbrowsing and, in turn, destroy themselves through starvation.

In the 1960s Luangua National Park in Zambia had a herd of an estimated 35,000 elephants. However, at that time they were unfortunately turning what had been a lush forest into a desert. Zimbabwe has just announced that it will have to remove approximately 5,000 elephants from their herds, estimated at 80,000, if they are to save the habitat. At least 50,000 elephants exist in Chobe National Park in Botswana, where they are wreaking havoc on the habitat due to their overabundance in a restricted region. Ordinarily, and traditionally, the elephants could have spread to other areas, but they are constantly being fenced in by the burgeoning human population.

The greatest boon to elephants today is the interest shown in them by people all over the world. As long as the native people can be recompensed by folks wanting to see and to photograph the elephants, or just to appreciate them from a distance, then the elephants have a very real value, and the future of these impressive, magnificent creatures can be assured.

The economic value of increased tourism has been a spur to conservation. This, coupled with an 80 percent decline in poaching, will allow herds to increase. In time, more and more large-tusked bulls will be seen.

INDEX

Page numbers in **bold-face** type indicate photo captions.